A Guide to Self-Publishing Your Christian Book

Maximizing the Ministry
Of the Printed Page

By Byron D. August

A Guide to Self-Publishing Your Christian Book: Maximizing the Ministry of the Printed Page
ISBN 0-9673727-3-9
Copyright © 2001 by Byron D. August
P. O. Box 2833
Broken Arrow, OK 74013

Editorial Consultant: Cynthia Hansen
P. O. Box 866
Broken Arrow, OK 74013

Cover Design: Dennis Whitley
1816 S. Umbrella Court
Broken Arrow, OK 74012

Text Design: Lisa Simpson, *Words Unlimited*
1432 W. Toledo
Broken Arrow, OK 74012

Contents

Introduction

I believe the printed page is a form of ministry that believers don't take advantage of as much as they should. Many Christians today have a message from God, but they lack an avenue through which to present that message to those who need to hear it. This is a sad state of affairs. It is so important that believers get the message God has placed in their hearts to the audience He intends for it to reach.

If you are in this situation, I believe you should prayerfully consider self-publishing your message in book form. The printed page will create a platform for you to get your God-given message out into the Body of Christ where it can bless people.

You see, the printed page can go places you will never be able to go. It can travel by air, land, or sea. It can penetrate all cultures, religions, races, and creeds. The printed page can bring your message into homes, schools, workplaces, and churches that you never dreamed would be recipients of what you have to say.

If the Lord Himself uses the printed page — the Bible — to present His message to the world, we should be willing to follow His example. The Bible has changed the world. It has been translated into a multitude of languages and has been around for centuries. God was printing His message long before there were printing presses around. He even wrote the Ten Commandments on stone and gave them to Moses for the deliverance of His people! If God uses the printed page to communicate with us, we should use it to communicate to His people as well.

The Lord spoke to a well-known minister years ago and told him that a large part of his worldwide ministry would be through the printed page. The Lord also told the minister that the printed page is one of the most effective ways to reach the world with the Gospel. I believe that is why God Himself uses this means by providing us with His written Word.

If you sense that the Lord is leading you to put into book form the message that is burning in your heart, I want to encourage you to pursue that goal with diligence. Don't let ignorance in the editorial and publishing field keep you from fulfilling that divine assignment!

That is what *A Guide to Self-Publishing Your Christian Book* is all about. This book is not an exhaustive study on the subject of self-publishing by any means. But I pray that it will provide the practical information you need not only to get the message in your heart onto the printed page, but to do it with excellence so that your message can bless and enrich many throughout the Body of Christ!

Byron D. August

How beautiful upon the mountains are the feet of him that bringeth good tidings, that PUBLISHETH peace; that bringeth good tidings of good, that PUBLISHETH salvation; that saith unto Zion, Thy God reigneth!

Isaiah 52:7

CHAPTER 1

Getting Your Message Onto the Printed Page

Perhaps a message from Heaven has been stirring in your heart for a while. You sense God's "nudge" on the inside of you to get that message out of your heart and onto the printed page so it can bless others as well. After praying about the matter, you finally come to the conclusion that self-publishing your own book is the route you are to go.

But how do you go about accomplishing that goal? What are the practical steps you must take to successfully self-publish your book? These are the questions I want to answer for you in this book.

Choosing a Marketable Subject

First of all, it is very important that you continue to pray for God's wisdom throughout the entire process of self-publishing your own book. You may face many challenges as you embark on this unfamiliar journey, but the Lord will give you wisdom to effectively handle every situation. As James 1:5 promises, *"If any of you lack wisdom, let him ask of God, that giveth to all men liberally, and upbraideth not; and it shall be given him."*

It also doesn't hurt to use a little common sense as you pursue your goal of self-publishing your own book. Therefore, before writing your manuscript, you should do what you can to choose a marketable subject.

Checking out your competition is a wise thing to do before writing your manuscript. If you find that a large quantity of books is already available to the Body of Christ on a particular subject, I would suggest that you consider writing on another subject. For instance, if the market is already flooded with books on faith, healing, prosperity, and the end times, it may be wise to choose another topic.

It is a good idea to conduct your own informal survey so you can find out what books are on the Christian market. Check to see what God is saying to the Body of Christ through His ministers. Go to at least ten bookstores and ask the clerk what books are in demand. What subjects are most requested by their customers?

Check out Christian magazines and Christian television to find out what subjects are predominantly being preached in churches. Contact publishing companies and ask what subjects they are currently accepting manuscripts for.

The Lord may want to use you to meet a great need in His Body regarding the printed page. For example, you may discover that certain denominations are in need of quality children's or youth material. Therefore, it's important to take the time to find out what type of printed material the Body of Christ is crying out for before you choose the topic of your book.

Before I began writing books, I personally took a survey to discover how many books on faith and healing were on the Christian market. Since I found a host of books on both subjects, I decided to pursue a different direction in choosing topics for my books.

You see, you want your book to stand out and be unique from the rest of the books on the market. This is especially important if you are not a well-known author or minister. Chances are that your book will not appeal to as many people as a book would that is written by one of the top ministers on the Christian scene today. Therefore, you want to find a subject:

- That will get people's attention.
- That will appeal to a large segment of the Body of Christ.
- For which there is a present need.
- That hasn't been adequately covered already.
- For which there is not much material available.

However, the most important thing is to be led by the Spirit of God when selecting a topic for your book. Don't discard the possibility that the Lord may lead you to write from a distinctive slant on a more common topic. And if you have already written your manuscript on one of these more common subjects, you may want to go back over it with this discussion in mind. Look for ways to put a different twist on your message or to approach the subject in a unique manner.

Who Should Write Your Book?

This may seem like an unusual question to ask in the process of self-publishing your book, but it is an important one nonetheless: You need to determine, "Who should write my book — me or a professional writer/editor?"

If you are skilled in the area of writing and know how to articulate your thoughts well through the written word, you should probably write your book yourself. Certainly it is more economical to do so because hiring a writer/editor to edit your written material costs less than hiring that same person to write your book.

On the other hand, writing may not be your gift. You may have no idea how to put your thoughts down in a way that is ordered and logical, yet interesting to the reader. In that case, you may want to consider hiring a professional Christian writer to help you get your message onto the printed page.

Perhaps you are more skilled at articulating yourself vocally than you are at writing down your thoughts. In that case, you may want to consider taping your message as you speak it out alone or before a live audience. You can then hire someone to transcribe the audiotape(s) word for word, exactly as you spoke out the message. These transcript(s) can be given to a professional writer who is skilled at crafting raw transcripts into a smooth, well-written book. The writer's objective should be to retain your voice and personality while articulating your message with accuracy and excellence on the printed page.

There is one more thing to consider before beginning to write your book. You need to decide which version of the Bible to use and what reference material you will utilize, if any. Check with your editor about whether or not you need to obtain written permission for certain versions of the Bible and any other reference books you decide to use. The editor should also be able to tell you how to proceed in obtaining that permission.

Ordering Necessary Forms

In order to self-publish your book, you will need to complete some important paperwork for the marketing and protection of your work. After you order these forms from the appropriate agency, you may not receive them for several weeks. Therefore, I suggest that you order all the necessary forms to publish your book while you are still writing your first draft or immediately after you have finished the first draft of your manuscript.

You will need to order the following forms (I recommend that you make photocopies of the completed forms before you mail them):

1. A copyright form is needed to obtain a copyright for your book so you can protect your material from infringement. The copyright notice is usually printed on the copyright page (on the back of the title page). To obtain a copyright form, you can write to Copyright Office, Library of Congress, Washington, D. C. 20599. You will need to complete the form, pay a fee, and send a few printed copies of your book to the Copyright Office.

2. If you want to make your book available to libraries, you will need to obtain a catalog card number for it. Write to the Library of Congress Cataloging In Publication Division, Washington, D. C. 20540-4320 to obtain information on obtaining a catalog card number.

3. You will also need to obtain an ISBN (International Standard Book Number) for your book. The ISBN is a ten-digit number that uniquely identifies books and book-like products that are

published internationally. The purpose of the ISBN is to uniquely identify one title or one edition of a title from one specific publisher. The ISBN allows for the more efficient marketing of products to booksellers, libraries, universities, wholesalers, and distributors. To apply for an ISBN, contact Standard Book Numbering Agency, R. R. Bowker Co., 121 Chanlon Road, New Providence, NJ 07974; (908) 665-6770.

4. You will also need to order a Bookland EAN bar code. The code provides for the ISBN to be printed in a worldwide compatible bar-code format. You can obtain a Bookland EAN bar code from several companies, a list of which should be in the information packet you receive when you apply for an ISBN with R. R. Bowker Co.

5. An advance book information (ABI) form will also be in your R. R. Bowker Co. information packet, along with your list of assigned ISBNs. You should fill out this ABI form so your book information will appear in *Books in Print*, a reference tool that lists books and book products published and distributed in the U. S. by more than 57,600 publishers.

The Editing Stage

Once the writing of your book is completed, your manuscript is ready to be edited. Throughout the writing stage, you should be praying and believing God to find the perfect person to edit your book.

You see, you want your book to flow smoothly and clearly so it will minister to the readers. However, it is almost impossible to accurately judge your own work. That's why I believe you should hire an editor to polish any written material you plan to publish and market. Your goal should be to publish your book with confidence, knowing that you did your best and hired the best so your material could be published with a high standard of excellence.

To bring your book to the highest level of excellence possible, your editor will address a host of potential editorial problems. Some of the things your editor will look for are grammatical errors, misspelled words, punctuation errors, inadequate chapter introductions and conclusions, and a lack of transitions between subjects and paragraphs. These are only a few of the problems your editor will address in a thorough edit of your manuscript.

In most cases, a good, well-seasoned Christian editor is on a tight time frame with several book projects lined up to work on at any given time. Therefore, try to make your editor's job as easy as possible. Before you submit your manuscript to the editor, ask him or her what you can do to help make the editing process go more smoothly.

It is important to get the price settled for editing your book before asking the editor to proceed. Most editors charge by the page, but prices for editing a book can vary. One determining factor is the amount of time and work that has to go into the manuscript. The more problems the editor needs to address in an edit, the more time that edit will take and the more money it will cost you.

It is also important to maintain a good line of communication with your editor. You should communicate to him or her the following:

- The primary purpose you wrote the book.
- The message you want to convey to the Body of Christ through your book.
- The audience you are trying to reach with that message.
- How much liberty the editor has to correct and revise your manuscript. (Personally, I like to find an editor I trust and then give him or her free course in the editing stage.)

After the editor completes an edit of your book, he or she will submit the first draft of the edited manuscript to you for your review. At this time, you should go over the manuscript carefully to see if you want to make any revisions or changes. This is the time to decide whether or not you want to clarify a point, to delete a sentence, to reword a phrase, etc. If you wait to make these types of changes until after the manuscript is typeset, you will make the typesetting process much more difficult for the typesetter and much more expensive for you.

You may also want to hire a professional proofreader at this stage to go over the edited manuscript as well, looking for misspelled words, grammatical or punctuation errors, word omissions, misquoted scripture references, etc.

After you have completed your first-draft review, the editor will make all the necessary corrections and return the final draft to you for your final approval. Carefully go over the final-draft manuscript one more time to make sure it is ready to be submitted to the typesetter.

The Typesetting and
Proofreading Stage

The typesetter sets up the text design to look the way you want it to in book form. By the end of the typesetting stage, the manuscript should be error-free and ready to go to the printer.

Most typesetters charge by the page. Shop around to find a good typesetter at a reasonable price. Remember, you will get what you pay for.

After you have selected a typesetter for your manuscript, you must decide on the style of text design for your book. Go to your local bookstore and check out the different styles that have been used in books already in print. When you find one or more text designs you like, bring examples to show your typesetter and discuss what style you would like for the various elements of your book.

Here are some of the elements of text design you will have to decide on:

- Type of font
- Point size of font
- Style of chapter and subtitle headings
- Style of running heads (alternating book title and chapter titles at the top of each page)
- Style of the table of contents page

Once you have chosen your text design format, your typesetter will typeset the book according to your specifications. After the manuscript has been typeset, a professional proofreader must go over it meticulously, looking for typing errors, misspellings, incorrect line breaks, spacing problems, style inconsistencies, etc.

The proofreading stage is a very important one because you want your book to be published at the highest level of quality possible. Check with your editor; he or she may want to be the one to proofread the manuscript to make sure every aspect of the book is editorially accurate.

Once the typeset manuscript is proofread, it is given back to the typesetter so he or she can insert all changes and corrections into the text. The manuscript should go back and forth between typesetter and proofreader until the proofreader has verified that all corrections have been accurately made.

After the book is finalized and print-ready, your typesetter should give you the typeset manuscript on computer disk, as well as a hard copy of the manuscript. This is one of your last opportunities to make any changes, so you should proofread the typeset manuscript several times to make sure it is free of all errors and exactly the way you want it to be printed. However, you need to realize that the typesetter will charge you a fee for any revisions you make at this stage (although you will probably not be charged for any typesetting errors you might catch).

It is wise to first discuss with your editor any revisions you want to make to the typeset manuscript. Also, after the typesetter has keyed in your revisions, make sure all changes have been checked by your editor. That way you can be confident that you have a finalized, print-ready manuscript and computer disk to give to the printer — the last step to take in getting your message onto the printed page!

CHAPTER 2

Determining the Layout
Of Your Book

L et's go back to the editing stage for a moment to discuss the initial layout of your book. Then we'll discuss some of the other layout decisions that have to be made at later stages of the self-publishing process.

Front Matter

Before your book can be typeset and printed, you first have to determine how you want the front and back matter arranged. Let's look at the front matter of the book first, which may consist of the following elements:

- Title page
- Copyright page
- Dedication
- Table of Contents
- Acknowledgments
- Foreword
- Preface
- Introduction

The *title page* normally consists of the book title and the author's name. It may also include the logo of your ministry or company.

The *copyright page* is usually on the reverse side of the title page. It should include:

- The primary Bible translations used in the book
- The edition or printing of the book (listed subsequent to the first edition or first printing)
- The title and author of the book
- The publisher's name and address (i.e., your ministry or company address)
- An International Standard Book Number (ISBN)
- The Library of Congress catalog number (if desired)
- Copyright information (e.g., "Printed in the United States of America. All rights reserved under International Copyright Law. Contents and/or cover may not be reproduced in whole or in part in any form without express written consent of the Publisher.")

The *dedication page* comes right before the table of contents page. You may or may not choose to dedicate your book to someone. For example, I dedicated my first book to my wife but chose to forego a dedication page in my second book.

The *table of contents* page is a very important element in your book. During a quick inspection of a new book, potential readers often go to the table of contents to find out what the book is about. Therefore, I suggest you keep your chapter titles short and descriptive. This makes it easier for your potential buyers to quickly grasp a general idea of the message you are conveying through your book.

The *acknowledgments page* provides an opportunity for the author to thank or acknowledge the individuals who helped make his or her book possible. Authors often acknowledge their family members, friends, coworkers, and those who assisted in getting the book in print.

A *foreword* is supposed to be written by someone whose own credibility in the reader's eyes can lend credibility to *you* and to your ability to write about the subject at hand. Therefore, a foreword written by someone who is well known and well respected can make your book much more marketable. Books that include a foreword may also be more appealing to a publishing company or a major book buyer.

A *preface* is the first opportunity the author has to personally address the reader and state his purpose for writing the book. Therefore, many readers go to the preface first to get a general idea of what the book is about and to find out what motivated and inspired the author to write his book.

Some authors also choose to include an *introduction*. An introduction does exactly that — introduces the overall message or theme of the book. It is an optional element, written by the author. In my first two books, I chose to include a preface but not an introduction; however, that decision is an option left entirely up to each individual author.

Back Matter

Now let's take a look at possible elements in the back matter of a book. These optional elements include:

- A "Prayer for Salvation" page
- An author's biography page
- A "For Further Information" page
- An "Other Books by Author" page (once you have more than one book in print)

A *"Prayer for Salvation" page* is appropriate to include in a scriptural teaching book as an avenue of ministry to the reader. If desired, you can replace this prayer with a specific prayer that applies to the message of your book.

The *author's biography page* is an excellent opportunity to let the reader get acquainted with you and with your credentials. You should include facts to reassure the reader that you have the knowledge and experience to address the subject of your book.

You may find that your credentials expand your book's appeal to a larger audience of readers. Here are a few suggestions of the type of facts you should let the reader know:

- Any titles you have earned (e.g., ordained minister, Ph.D., etc.)
- Your level of education
- Your work experience
- Your ministerial or occupational achievements
- The names of your family members (spouse and children) and where you reside

It is a great idea to include a *"For Further Information" page* at the back of your book. The following is an example of what this information page could say:

**For additional copies of this book
or for more information
regarding [author's name] ministry schedule,
please write the address below:
[insert personal, ministry,
or company address]**

This page provides an important means of advertisement for you. It is also an effective way to let your readers know where they can write to order more copies of your book, to give you their feedback on the book or their prayer requests, or to contact you to schedule a meeting (if you are a minister or traveling speaker).

An *"Other Books by Author" page* is another optional means of advertisement for you as an author. The reader who has been ministered to by your book may be very interested in learning about other books you have written. However, I suggest that you only include a list of your other books if you have written at least three books in all.

Your Book's Cover Design

Also included in determining the layout of your book is your choice of a cover design.

A good-looking cover is a very important marketing tool. You can have a great book, but if the cover isn't appealing, it can greatly reduce the number of books you sell. Therefore, you should want your book to stand out from the rest that are on the market.

Hiring a good graphic artist is a very important step in introducing your book to the world. Therefore, make sure you are led by the Holy Spirit as you look for a graphic designer so you can obtain the best-looking, most impactful book cover possible.

The best time for you to contact a graphic artist about designing your book cover is right after you have completed writing your book. That way he or she can work on the cover design while the manuscript goes through the editing and typesetting stages.

You don't want your graphic artist to guess what you want your book cover to look like. Therefore, to help him get started, you should provide him with ideas or possible examples of cover designs you like. Let him know if you have any specific designs or pictures you want to incorporate in the cover design. Also, don't hesitate to draw on the artist's expertise; be open to any suggestions he may have on the subject.

Most book covers include a graphic design, the title (and subtitle, if any), and the author's name. You may also want to include on the front cover the name of the person who wrote your foreword. If this person is well known, you can enhance the book's credibility as well as its sale potential by including his or her name. However, make sure you tell the artist you want to do this before he begins working on the cover concept(s).

In fact, you should make sure that you provide the artist with *all* the information he needs to design the book cover before he begins the project. This should include:

- The book title
- The book manuscript (needed so the artist can skim the contents while determining an appropriate cover concept)

- The colors you prefer to be used for the book cover
- Any other pertinent information that could steer the designing process in the right direction

Besides telling the artist *which* colors you would prefer for your book cover, let him also know *how many* colors you want him to use. Many authors decide to go with a four-color cover, which is more expensive to print than a two-color cover but much more attractive to the reader's eye.

All these factors are very important to consider because a good cover design will draw readers to your book. I know this from experience, having purchased books myself because I loved their covers. Your cover can even draw people to your book who may not be interested in the subject you are writing about. Your cover will either enhance or hurt sales, so don't sacrifice quality to get a cheaper price for your cover design. Do your very best to find someone who can design an excellent book cover with which to present your book to the world.

Most graphic artists will provide at least two or three cover design concepts for a set fee. Once you have chosen the cover design you prefer, the artist will prepare the front cover, spine, and back cover for printing.

The book cover's spine normally includes the book title, the author's name, and the publisher's logo. The artist won't be able to finalize the spine size until he knows the final page count of the typeset manuscript.

The spine is important because it provides the reader easy access to the book title and author's name while the book sits on the bookshelf of a store or library.

Some book-selling companies will only carry books that are large enough to have a spine. Keep this in mind when you are discussing the cover design with your graphic artist.

The back cover usually includes a few paragraphs describing the book's contents in a way that catches the reader's interest. It can also include your picture, along with a short version of your author's biography. You should supply all this information (after it is edited by your editor) to your graphic artist on a computer disc so he can include it in the back cover design.

After the front and back cover is completed, your editor or proofreader should proofread the cover to make sure it is error-free. Then the artist will provide a disc that includes art files, spine measurements, and all other information the printer needs to produce the book cover.

Ready To Print

Once you have hard copies and disk copies of your edited, typeset manuscript and of your book cover artwork, your book is ready to print. Shop around for quotes from a variety of printers. (For example, before I chose a printer, I obtained ten quotes from ten different printers.) Believe God to direct you to a good printer with reasonable rates.

During the process of selecting a printer, ask to see some of the books and other products printed by the company so you can ascertain the quality of its work. Also, ask each printer if the company provides the client with the film of the printed book at the completion of the printing (some printers do not). Select a printer that will take care not only of printing and binding the book, but also of packaging and delivering the printed copies to your chosen destination. (If you choose an out-of-state printer, you may have to pay for the shipping.)

A printing company will need to know certain facts about the project and several layout decisions you have made before they can give you an accurate quote for printing your book. For instance, the printer will probably ask for the following information:

- The quantity of books you want to print
- The trim size of the pages
- The final page count (***Note***: Blank pages may need to be added at the back of the book so the page count will match one of the standard book sizes used in printing, called a "signature.")
- The type, size, and weight of paper you want to use both for your cover and for the pages of your book
- The number of colors to be used in your cover design
- The color of font used in your body text
- The type of protective coating you want on your cover
- The kind of binding your book is to have

Let me mention here the two primary methods of binding a book. My first book is a "perfect-bound book." In other words, its cover is glued to its pages. This is the most common form of binding for larger, soft-bound books with a spine.

My second book is smaller and therefore "saddle-stitched." A saddle-stitched book doesn't have a spine and is therefore stapled directly on its center fold.

Books that are less than quarter-inch thick or less than 64 pages are normally saddle-stitched.

The printer may need more information than what is listed above. But if he knows these key facts about your book, he can at least get started in calculating an estimated price for printing your book.

Once you have selected your printer, make sure the contract you sign with the company spells out the agreed-upon price. Also, ask the printer to return the computer disks containing your typeset manuscript and book cover artwork after the printing process is completed. These disks can be used for future print runs.

We have looked at some of the layout decisions that must be made from start to finish in the publishing process. As you make these decisions that determine what your book will look like and how it will be arranged, don't hesitate to call upon the expertise of the professionals you are working with at each stage of the process. Their experience in making these types of decisions will serve you well in producing the most polished finished product possible.

CHAPTER 3

Tips on Successfully Marketing Your Book

You can market your book with confidence when you have a marketable title, a great-looking cover, and a competitive price.

A competitive price is a very important factor in your marketing scheme. You can significantly hurt your sales by overpricing your book. Therefore, before signing a contract with a printer, you should conduct another informal survey in several bookstores to check out the price range of books of similar size that are written on similar topics.

For instance, suppose your book has 80 pages, and you find that 80-page books are priced between $6.99 and $7.99. Use that information to help determine the price of your own book as you calculate the costs of production.

Establishing a Competitive Price

I recommend that you sell your book at a price that is $1.00 or $2.00 lower than similar books on the market written by famous or well-established authors. People tend to buy material from authors who are well known more readily than they do from an author they have never heard of before.

Also, keep in mind that you will have to sell your book to bookstores at a discount price so they can make a profit as well. The standard wholesale discount is normally 40% off the retail price of the book. For instance, if the retail price is $6.99, the wholesale price to bookstores would be $4.19. In that case, the total cost to produce each book would have to be less than $4.19 in order for you to make a profit.

I believe a profit margin of $2.00 to $3.00 for each book is a reasonable profit. If you can make a larger margin of profit, that is even better. So if your wholesale price is $4.19 and you want to make $2.00 to $3.00 profit per book, you will need to produce each book for $2.19 or less.

To accomplish this goal, establish an expense budget and try not to exceed it. If you want to have a reasonably-priced book, your goal should be to keep the production costs as low as possible while maintaining a high standard of quality.

About 70% of your budget will go toward the cost of printing your book. So if your expense budget includes $5,000.00 to spend on publishing your book, designate at least $3,500.00 for printing and the other $1,500.00 for your other publishing expenses. (**Note:** These figures would have to be adjusted if a professional writer wrote your book from raw transcripts, as discussed earlier.)

To calculate your total cost to produce each book, add together the cost of each production stage. This would include the cost of:

- Editing
- Proofreading the edited manuscript
- Typesetting
- Proofreading the typeset manuscript
- Cover design
- ISBN fee
- Bar code fee
- Copyright fee
- Printing

Let's say the cost of all these stages add up to $5,000.00. If you divide this amount by the number of books to be printed, you will arrive at your cost per book.

Let's look at an example of a budget expense sheet to help illustrate what I am saying.

Budget Expense Sheet

Cost to print 5,000 books	$4,000.00
Editing	$ 768.00
1st Proofreading (optional)	$ 160.00
Typesetting	$ 280.00
2nd Proofreading	$ 160.00
Graphic artist	$ 400.00
ISBN fee	$ 20.00
Bookland bar code fee	$ 25.00
Copyright fee	$ 20.00
TOTAL BOOK EXPENSE:	$5,833.00

In this hypothetical situation, the total cost to produce 5,000 books is $5,833.00. When you divide $5,833.00 into 5,000, you arrive at your cost to produce each book — in this case, $1.16 per book.

The important thing to remember is to keep your costs to produce your book as low as possible without sacrificing quality. The higher your costs of production, the higher you will have to raise the book price.

Remember, you need to make a profit. If you have to price your book higher than other books on the market that have a similar topic and page count, your books may not sell as quickly as you would like them to.

Let's go back to our example. Your cost per book is $1.16, and you are considering a market retail price of $6.99. Bookstores will purchase your books at the wholesale discount, which is 40% off the retail price. In this case, the wholesale price to bookstores would be $4.19. When you subtract your production cost per book from your wholesale price per book ($4.19 - $1.16), you find out that your profit on each book is $3.03 per book, while the bookstores make a profit of $2.80 per book, plus sales tax.

If you sell all 5,000 books in your inventory for $4.19 each, your sales will total $20,950. When you subtract your total cost of production ($5,833.00) from your total sales ($20,950.00), your profit margin is $15,117.00 (minus any advertising costs you incur after production).

Advertising and Distribution

How you advertise and market your book is an important factor in determining the success of your book sales. You have to let the world know about your book if you want to sell it. (***Note:*** Keep good records of every book sale for tax purposes. You should contact your CPA for more information.)

Make it your goal to get your book in the hands of key people who will talk about it. You want to get as many people talking about your book as possible.

Sometimes your family and friends can be your best source of advertising and marketing. Therefore, I suggest that you send out complimentary copies of your book to family members and friends as soon as they are printed. Giving complimentary copies to bookstores, churches, libraries, and book distributors will also help you market your title.

You should use any means of advertisement that avails itself to you. Below is a list of advertising methods you may want to consider when planning a marketing strategy for your book:

1. Television
2. Radio
3. Newspapers
4. Magazines
5. Internet
6. Public speaking meetings
7. Conduct book-signing sessions at local bookstores.
8. Display your book in restaurants, hotels, and grocery stores.
9. Attend book publishing conferences that attract bookstore owners and book buyers.
10. Ask your pastor or another personal acquaintance of influence to write a review on your book to submit to the local newspaper for possible publication.

TELEVISION

You should take advantage of any opportunity that presents itself for a television appearance. Find out what local Christian stations are in your area. Many Christian television ministries frequently conduct free interviews with authors, so it is always worthwhile to inquire about this possibility.

Also, call your local television stations and find out if they offer any opportunities to new authors. For instance, you may find a news station that is willing to give new authors exposure by mentioning them when their first book is published.

If an opportunity arises for your book to gain exposure by means of television, don't fail to take advantage of that opportunity. You may only be offered a 15-minute interview, but that short interview could result in sales that make the endeavor well worth your effort.

Before your interview, the talk show host may have you write down some pertinent questions that he or she can ask you about your book. Some hosts may choose to conduct a preliminary interview a few hours before the actual television interview to serve as a "practice run."

Before your scheduled appearance on a television program, find out the entire area the broadcast will cover. Then communicate with the area pastors and bookstore owners to let them know about your television interview and your book. This may be an open door for you to put your books on their shelves.

RADIO

Your local Christian radio station can be a great avenue for marketing your book. Therefore, find out if the station has a talk show that conducts free interviews with Christians of interest in the local community.

If you are a minister, you may even want to inquire about ministering on the radio. A radio program can provide an opportunity not only to teach the Word, but to market your book to the listener. However, it is a good idea to first ask the radio station if it has any rules or guidelines concerning advertising before or after you minister the Word.

Purchasing time for your own radio advertisement is also a great way to market your book. However, some Christian radio stations may only offer advertising to churches and ministries. If individual advertising is allowed, check first to see what the station has to offer before you agree to the terms. For instance, find out if your ad would receive full network coverage.

You should know exactly what you want to say before you actually record your advertisement. Keep in mind that your ad must fit in the amount of time you purchase. If your purchased time is short, it would be wise to keep the ad as simple as possible. For instance, you may just want to give the listener a brief excerpt from your book, its price, and where it can be purchased.

LOCAL NEWSPAPERS

Your local newspaper is another potential avenue for marketing your book. As a local author of a brand-new book, you are news to a lot of people in the community. Therefore, bring your book to the attention of someone at the newspaper who is eager for a great story.

You should check your local newspaper to see if it includes a section for interviews with local authors. If it does, contact that particular department of the newspaper and see if there is any interest in conducting an interview with you regarding your new book.

If your local newspaper doesn't offer these types of interviews, check to see if it includes feature articles about local people. If so, contact the appropriate department and inquire regarding the possibility of a feature article being written about you and your new book.

MAGAZINES

Purchasing ads in Christian magazines can be a very effective means of marketing your book and giving it exposure to the Body of Christ. Although the cost to advertise in some magazines may seem high, in the end this type of advertising could pay rich dividends to you in book sales.

There are many Christian magazines on the market today that allow individuals to purchase ads. Contact the magazine with which you want to advertise and ask to speak with the advertising department. When you ask for more details on advertising your book, be sure to ask relevant questions about the magazine that will help you gauge the effectiveness of advertising in that particular magazine. For instance, ask how many homes the magazine goes to every month, since that information is certainly relevant to the number of potential book sales.

LOCAL CHRISTIAN BOOKSTORES

You should contact every Christian bookstore in your community and tell the bookstore owners about your book. I suggest that you develop a good working relationship with these owners even before your book is released. If a bookstore owner knows who you are, that personal contact can make a big difference in determining whether or not your book ends up on his store shelves.

Some bookstores may accept your book just because you are a local author. However, two other very important factors can work in your favor: 1) maintaining a professional appearance; and 2) making sure you have a great-looking cover on the book.

Some bookstore owners will tell you that they only accept books through a major distributor. If you have signed with a Christian distributor (*see* discussion on pages 38-39), let these owners know from what company they can purchase your books.

If your books are not available through a major distributor, you may be able to set up a consignment account with a bookstore owner. This type of account presents no risk to the bookstore owner because books that are accepted on consignment require no up-front costs.

When your books are on consignment, you do not receive any payment from the owner until your books sell. You and the bookstore owner will have to agree on the time frame of payment and the division of profit percentages for books that are sold. Many stores keep 30% to 40% of a consignment book's retail price. A fair profit division to adopt is 60% to the author and 40% to the bookstore.

Once a store has accepted your book, I recommend that you ask the owner about the possibility of setting up a book-signing date. A book-signing session provides an excellent way to increase book sales beyond what you could achieve if your book just sat on the bookstore shelf amongst hundreds of other books.

A book-signing can also provide great exposure for your book and for you as a new author. Besides the contacts you make on the actual book-signing date, you will also receive free advertising in the form of posters in the bookstore windows that display your picture and excerpts from your book. (The store may or may not be willing to pay for more expanded methods of advertising your book-signing session.)

Local Businesses

Any place of business where you are a regular customer presents a potential opportunity for you to display your books. Some businesses may agree to your request because you have developed a good relationship with the owner or manager; others may agree because they don't want to risk losing your business.

So contact the restaurants you regularly frequent, the grocery stores you shop at every week, and any other place of business where you have established a good relationship with someone in charge, such as beauty shops, car dealerships, hotels, convenience stores, dry cleaners, doctor's offices, etc. One rule of thumb I follow in deciding which businesses to approach is this: Any place of business that allows a vendor machine is a potential place for me to display my books.

You just have to be willing to go in and talk to the business owners about displaying your books. Remember, the goal of most businessmen is to make money, so you need to prepare a marketing presentation that convinces the business owner of his potential profit in granting your request. (However, you may encounter some business owners who don't require a percentage of the profits. They may just decide to display your books as a blessing to you and let you keep all the profit.)

Try to get your books in the door, so to speak, even if it means agreeing to give the owner 50% of the retail price of any book sold. That kind of sacrifice may prove to be worthwhile to you in the months to come.

LIBRARIES

Making your book known to your local library is another way to generate publicity and sales. Some libraries have set up a program of scheduled meetings where local authors speak about their books to interested attendees. Contact your local library to see if such a program exists in your community.

In addition, there are companies that will market your book to libraries across the country. You can obtain information about these companies from your local library. You will probably be charged a fee for this service, but the cost could prove to be a sound investment. This type of company provides a means for you to get your book into libraries nationwide — a goal that could not be achieved on your own.

INTERNET

The internet is another effective avenue through which to market and sell your book. There are several successful companies that sell books to people all over the world on the internet. You may be able to market your book through one or more of these companies, with the company keeping a certain percentage of the book's retail price.

When you find the company or companies with which you want to do business, you should be able to go to the company's website and complete the application online. On the application, you will have to provide information about yourself or your company, as well as about your book (e.g., a short summary of the contents, the target audience, the book's retail price, etc.).

Once your application is accepted, it may take a few days for the company to get your book ready for sale over the internet. When it is ready, the company will probably contact you by e-mail to let you know the status of your account.

SIGNING WITH A DISTRIBUTOR

Signing a contract with a book distributor is another avenue you can use to market and sell your books. A distributing company will keep a large portion of your proceeds for its services. However, signing with a major Christian distributor can be beneficial because your book will be displayed in a variety of places that would otherwise be off limits to you.

Most distributors will work with you on a consignment basis. The company will let you know the terms of their distribution services; then you can try to negotiate any terms you might want to include in your agreement.

Once you reach an agreement with a distributor, you will probably be asked to ship the company a certain number of books. The distributor will then make your books available to a wide variety of customers.

Some of the large chain bookstores, both secular and Christian, will not stock your book on their shelves because their store has a policy to buy only from certain distributors. Most bookstores will let you know which distributors they do business with.

This list of marketing methods that we've discussed is certainly not exhaustive, but it does give you a good idea of some of the marketing options available to you as a publisher of your own book. I recommend that you stay diversified in your marketing and distribution strategies. And of course, through it all you should keep this one principle in mind: Seek God for wisdom, and endeavor to be led by His Spirit in each decision you make.

One Step at a Time
Toward Your Goal

I pray that this book has been a blessing to you and will assist you in your writing endeavors. Remember to take one step at a time, and refuse to get discouraged. You will face many challenges when you decide to become an author. But the Lord will be there by your side to help you every step of the way.

Galatians 6:9 says, *"...Let us not be weary in well doing: for in due season we shall reap, if we faint not."* You may have some great opportunities to give up and quit as you work toward self-publishing your book. But if the Lord has told you to get your message out in print, you must endure every test, trial, and obstacle that tries to stand in your way.

Many people faint right before their "due season" — their time of harvest when they are rewarded with success for obeying God. Don't make that same mistake.

When obstacles arise — whether it is the lack of finances, people's negative opinions, or your own thoughts of self-doubt — remember that the Holy Spirit is leading you through this entire process. Just keep following your heart's dream, and do what the Lord has called you to do. Get your message onto the printed page, where it can begin to bless the world with its life-changing truth!

About the Author

Rev. Byron August was born in 1964 in Donaldsonville, Louisiana, and at the age of eight, accepted Jesus Christ as his Savior. Inspired by his grandmother, Rev. August began a life of serving and has been very active in the helps ministry ever since.

When Rev. August was 18 years old, he began attending a Full Gospel church. Eager to embrace every opportunity to serve people, Rev. August performed janitorial duties, worked in the church bookstore, and visited nursing homes and jails. After proving himself faithful to serve, he was appointed to oversee various areas of the church's helps ministry and outreach programs. In addition to these duties, Rev. August also taught a Sunday school class and served as a deacon in the church.

In 1984, Rev. August graduated from Nicholls State University in Thibodaux, Louisiana, with an Associate of Science degree in general business. In 1992, he took a sixteen-month sabbatical to serve as a missionary to Lima, Peru, in South America. While on the mission field, Rev. August ministered in various churches throughout the country, taught in a local Bible school, and worked in a local missions station. He also met and married his wife, Dr. Sylvia August, who now serves alongside him in the ministry.

Rev. August is a licensed itinerant minister who conducts services throughout the United States and Latin America. He is also the author of other books, including *How To Be the Greatest in God's Kingdom* and *Are You Profitable to Your Pastor?* He and his wife Sylvia reside in Broken Arrow, Oklahoma, with their children, Daniel and Victoria.

For Further Information

For additional copies of this book
or for further information regarding
Rev. August's ministry schedule,
please write:

Rev. Byron August
P. O. Box 2833
Broken Arrow, OK 74013